Poems by Emily Brontë

Emily Brontë

CONTENTS

A Little While, A Little While

A LITTLE while, a little while,
The weary task is put away,
And I can sing and I can smile,
Alike, while I have holiday.

Where wilt thou go, my harassed heart—
What thought, what scene invites thee now
What spot, or near or far apart,
Has rest for thee, my weary brow?

There is a spot, 'mid barren hills,
Where winter howls, and driving rain;
But, if the dreary tempest chills,
There is a light that warms again.

The house is old, the trees are bare,
Moonless above bends twilight's dome;
But what on earth is half so dear—
So longed for—as the hearth of home?

The mute bird sitting on the stone,
The dank moss dripping from the wall,
The thorn-trees gaunt, the walks o'ergrown,
I love them—how I love them all!

Still, as I mused, the naked room,
The alien firelight died away;
And from the midst of cheerless gloom,
I passed to bright, unclouded day.

A little and a lone green lane
That opened on a common wide;
A distant, dreamy, dim blue chain
Of mountains circling every side.

A heaven so clear, an earth so calm,
So sweet, so soft, so hushed an air;
And, deepening still the dream-like charm,
Wild moor-sheep feeding everywhere.

THAT was the scene, I knew it well;
I knew the turfy pathway's sweep,
That, winding o'er each billowy swell,
Marked out the tracks of wandering sheep.

Could I have lingered but an hour,
It well had paid a week of toil;
But Truth has banished Fancy's power:
Restraint and heavy task recoil.

Even as I stood with raptured eye,
Absorbed in bliss so deep and dear,
My hour of rest had fleeted by,
And back came labour, bondage, care.

A Daydream

1846

On a sunny brae alone I lay
One summer afternoon;
It was the marriage-time of May,
With her young lover, June.

From her mother's heart seemed loath to part
That queen of bridal charms,
But her father smiled on the fairest child
He ever held in his arms.

The trees did wave their plumy crests,
The glad birds carolled clear;
And I, of all the wedding guests,
Was only sullen there!

There was not one, but wished to shun
My aspect void of cheer;
The very gray rocks, looking on,
Asked, "What do you here?"

And I could utter no reply;
In sooth, I did not know
Why I had brought a clouded eye
To greet the general glow.

So, resting on a heathy bank,
I took my heart to me;
And we together sadly sank
Into a reverie.
We thought, "When winter comes again,
Where will these bright things be?
All vanished, like a vision vain,
An unreal mockery!

"The birds that now so blithely sing,
Through deserts, frozen dry,
Poor spectres of the perished spring,
In famished troops will fly.

"And why should we be glad at all?
The leaf is hardly green,
Before a token of its fall
Is on the surface seen!"

Now, whether it were really so,
I never could be sure;
But as in fit of peevish woe,
I stretched me on the moor,

A thousand thousand gleaming fires
Seemed kindling in the air;
A thousand thousand silvery lyres
Resounded far and near:

Methought, the very breath I breathed
Was full of sparks divine,
And all my heather-couch was wreathed
By that celestial shine!

And, while the wide earth echoing rung
To that strange minstrelsy
The little glittering spirits sung,
Or seemed to sing, to me:

"O mortal! mortal! let them die;
Let time and tears destroy,
That we may overflow the sky
With universal joy!

"Let grief distract the sufferer's breast,
And night obscure his way;
They hasten him to endless rest,

And everlasting day.

"To thee the world is like a tomb,
A desert's naked shore;
To us, in unimagined bloom,
It brightens more and more!

"And, could we lift the veil, and give
One brief glimpse to thine eye,
Thou wouldst rejoice for those that live,
BECAUSE they live to die."

The music ceased; the noonday dream,
Like dream of night, withdrew;
But Fancy, still, will sometimes deem
Her fond creation true.

A Death-scene

1846

"O day! he cannot die
When thou so fair art shining!
O Sun, in such a glorious sky,
So tranquilly declining;

He cannot leave thee now,
While fresh west winds are blowing,
And all around his youthful brow
Thy cheerful light is glowing!

Edward, awake, awake—
The golden evening gleams
Warm and bright on Arden's lake—
Arouse thee from thy dreams!

Beside thee, on my knee,
My dearest friend, I pray
That thou, to cross the eternal sea,
Wouldst yet one hour delay:

I hear its billows roar—
I see them foaming high;
But no glimpse of a further shore
Has blest my straining eye.

Believe not what they urge
Of Eden isles beyond;
Turn back, from that tempestuous surge,
To thy own native land.
It is not death, but pain
That struggles in thy breast—
Nay, rally, Edward, rouse again;
I cannot let thee rest!"

One long look, that sore reproved me
For the woe I could not bear—
One mute look of suffering moved me
To repent my useless prayer:

And, with sudden check, the heaving
Of distraction passed away;
Not a sign of further grieving
Stirred my soul that awful day.

Paled, at length, the sweet sun setting;
Sunk to peace the twilight breeze:
Summer dews fell softly, wetting
Glen, and glade, and silent trees.

Then his eyes began to weary,
Weighed beneath a mortal sleep;
And their orbs grew strangely dreary,
Clouded, even as they would weep.

But they wept not, but they changed not,
Never moved, and never closed;
Troubled still, and still they ranged not—
Wandered not, nor yet reposed!

So I knew that he was dying—
Stooped, and raised his languid head;
Felt no breath, and heard no sighing,
So I knew that he was dead.

Anticipation

How beautiful the earth is still,
To thee—how full of happiness?
How little fraught with real ill,
Or unreal phantoms of distress!
How spring can bring thee glory, yet,
And summer win thee to forget
December's sullen time!
Why dost thou hold the treasure fast,
Of youth's delight, when youth is past,
And thou art near thy prime?

When those who were thy own compeers,
Equals in fortune and in years,
Have seen their morning melt in tears,
To clouded, smileless day;
Blest, had they died untried and young,
Before their hearts went wandering wrong,—
Poor slaves, subdued by passions strong,
A weak and helpless prey!

'Because, I hoped while they enjoyed,
And by fulfilment, hope destroyed;
As children hope, with trustful breast,
I waited bliss—and cherished rest.
A thoughtful spirit taught me soon,
That we must long till life be done;
That every phase of earthly joy
Must always fade, and always cloy:

'This I foresaw—and would not chase
The fleeting treacheries;
But, with firm foot and tranquil face,
Held backward from that tempting race,
Gazed o'er the sands the waves efface,
To the enduring seas—

There cast my anchor of desire
Deep in unknown eternity;
Nor ever let my spirit tire,
With looking for WHAT IS TO BE!

"It is hope's spell that glorifies,
Like youth, to my maturer eyes,
All Nature's million mysteries,
The fearful and the fair—
Hope soothes me in the griefs I know;
She lulls my pain for others' woe,
And makes me strong to undergo
What I am born to bear.

Glad comforter! will I not brave,
Unawed, the darkness of the grave?
Nay, smile to hear Death's billows rave—
Sustained, my guide, by thee?
The more unjust seems present fate,
The more my spirit swells elate,
Strong, in thy strength, to anticipate
Rewarding destiny!

Death

Death! that struck when I was most confiding.
In my certain faith of joy to be—
Strike again, Time's withered branch dividing
From the fresh root of Eternity!

Leaves, upon Time's branch, were growing brightly,
Full of sap, and full of silver dew;
Birds beneath its shelter gathered nightly;
Daily round its flowers the wild bees flew.

Sorrow passed, and plucked the golden blossom;
Guilt stripped off the foliage in its pride
But, within its parent's kindly bosom,
Flowed for ever Life's restoring tide.

Little mourned I for the parted gladness,
For the vacant nest and silent song—
Hope was there, and laughed me out of sadness;
Whispering, "Winter will not linger long!"

And, behold! with tenfold increase blessing,
Spring adorned the beauty-burdened spray;
Wind and rain and fervent heat, caressing,
Lavished glory on that second May!

High it rose—no winged grief could sweep it;
Sin was scared to distance with its shine;
Love, and its own life, had power to keep it
From all wrong—from every blight but thine!

Cruel Death! The young leaves droop and languish;
Evening's gentle air may still restore—
No! the morning sunshine mocks my anguish-
Time, for me, must never blossom more!

Strike it down, that other boughs may flourish
Where that perished sapling used to be;
Thus, at least, its mouldering corpse will nourish
That from which it sprung—Eternity.

Encouragement

I do not weep; I would not weep;
Our mother needs no tears:
Dry thine eyes, too; 'tis vain to keep
This causeless grief for years.

What though her brow be changed and cold,
Her sweet eyes closed for ever?
What though the stone — the darksome mould
Our mortal bodies sever?

What though her hand smooth ne'er again
Those silken locks of thine?
Nor, through long hours of future pain,
Her kind face o'er thee shine?

Remember still, she is not dead;
She sees us, sister, now;
Laid, where her angel spirit fled,
'Mid heath and frozen snow.

And from that world of heavenly light
Will she not always bend
To guide us in our lifetime's night,
And guard us to the end?

Thou knowest she will; and thou mayst mourn
That WE are left below:
But not that she can ne'er return
To share our earthly woe.

Faith And Despondency

"The winter wind is loud and wild,
Come close to me, my darling child;
Forsake thy books, and mateless play;
And, while the night is gathering gray,
We'll talk its pensive hours away;—

"Ierne, round our sheltered hall
November's gusts unheeded call;
Not one faint breath can enter here
Enough to wave my daughter's hair,
And I am glad to watch the blaze
Glance from her eyes, with mimic rays;
To feel her cheek, so softly pressed,
In happy quiet on my breast,

"But, yet, even this tranquillity
Brings bitter, restless thoughts to me;
And, in the red fire's cheerful glow,
I think of deep glens, blocked with snow;
I dream of moor, and misty hill,
Where evening closes dark and chill;
For, lone, among the mountains cold,
Lie those that I have loved of old.
And my heart aches, in hopeless pain,
Exhausted with repinings vain,
That I shall greet them ne'er again!"

"Father, in early infancy,
When you were far beyond the sea,
Such thoughts were tyrants over me!
I often sat, for hours together,
Through the long nights of angry weather,
Raised on my pillow, to descry
The dim moon struggling in the sky;
Or, with strained ear, to catch the shock,

Of rock with wave, and wave with rock;
So would I fearful vigil keep,
And, all for listening, never sleep.
But this world's life has much to dread,
Not so, my Father, with the dead.

"Oh! not for them, should we despair,
The grave is drear, but they are not there;
Their dust is mingled with the sod,
Their happy souls are gone to God!
You told me this, and yet you sigh,
And murmur that your friends must die.
Ah! my dear father, tell me why?
For, if your former words were true,
How useless would such sorrow be;
As wise, to mourn the seed which grew
Unnoticed on its parent tree,
Because it fell in fertile earth,
And sprang up to a glorious birth—
Struck deep its root, and lifted high
Its green boughs in the breezy sky.

"But, I'll not fear, I will not weep
For those whose bodies rest in sleep,—
I know there is a blessed shore,
Opening its ports for me and mine;
And, gazing Time's wide waters o'er,
I weary for that land divine,
Where we were born, where you and I
Shall meet our dearest, when we die;
From suffering and corruption free,
Restored into the Deity."
"Well hast thou spoken, sweet, trustful child!
And wiser than thy sire;
And worldly tempests, raging wild,
Shall strengthen thy desire—
Thy fervent hope, through storm and foam,
Through wind and ocean's roar,

To reach, at last, the eternal home,
The steadfast, changeless shore!"

Honour's Martyr

The moon is full this winter night;
The stars are clear, though few;
And every window glistens bright
With leaves of frozen dew.

The sweet moon through your lattice gleams,
And lights your room like day;
And there you pass, in happy dreams,
The peaceful hours away!

While I, with effort hardly quelling
The anguish in my breast,
Wander about the silent dwelling,
And cannot think of rest.

The old clock in the gloomy hall
Ticks on, from hour to hour;
And every time its measured call
Seems lingering slow and slower:

And, oh, how slow that keen-eyed star
Has tracked the chilly gray!
What, watching yet! how very far
The morning lies away!

Without your chamber door I stand;
Love, are you slumbering still?
My cold heart, underneath my hand,
Has almost ceased to thrill.

Bleak, bleak the east wind sobs and sighs,
And drowns the turret bell,
Whose sad note, undistinguished, dies
Unheard, like my farewell!

To-morrow, Scorn will blight my name,
And Hate will trample me,
Will load me with a coward's shame—
A traitor's perjury.

False friends will launch their covert sneers;
True friends will wish me dead;
And I shall cause the bitterest tears
That you have ever shed.

The dark deeds of my outlawed race
Will then like virtues shine;
And men will pardon their disgrace,
Beside the guilt of mine.

For, who forgives the accursed crime
Of dastard treachery?
Rebellion, in its chosen time,
May Freedom's champion be;

Revenge may stain a righteous sword,
It may be just to slay;
But, traitor, traitor,—from THAT word
All true breasts shrink away!

Oh, I would give my heart to death,
To keep my honour fair;
Yet, I'll not give my inward faith
My honour's NAME to spare!

Not even to keep your priceless love,
Dare I, Beloved, deceive;
This treason should the future prove,
Then, only then, believe!

I know the path I ought to go
I follow fearlessly,

Inquiring not what deeper woe
Stern duty stores for me.

So foes pursue, and cold allies
Mistrust me, every one:
Let me be false in others' eyes,
If faithful in my own.

Hope

Hope Was but a timid friend;
She sat without the grated den,
Watching how my fate would tend,
Even as selfish-hearted men.

She was cruel in her fear;
Through the bars one dreary day,
I looked out to see her there,
And she turned her face away!

Like a false guard, false watch keeping,
Still, in strife, she whispered peace;
She would sing while I was weeping;
If I listened, she would cease.

False she was, and unrelenting;
When my last joys strewed the ground,
Even Sorrow saw, repenting,
Those sad relics scattered round;

Hope, whose whisper would have given
Balm to all my frenzied pain,
Stretched her wings, and soared to heaven,
Went, and ne'er returned again!

How Clear She Shines

How clear she shines! How quietly
I lie beneath her guardian light;
While heaven and earth are whispering me,
"To morrow, wake, but dream to-night."
Yes, Fancy, come, my Fairy love!
These throbbing temples softly kiss;
And bend my lonely couch above,
And bring me rest, and bring me bliss.

The world is going; dark world, adieu!
Grim world, conceal thee till the day;
The heart thou canst not all subdue
Must still resist, if thou delay!

Thy love I will not, will not share;
Thy hatred only wakes a smile;
Thy griefs may wound—thy wrongs may tear,
But, oh, thy lies shall ne'er beguile!
While gazing on the stars that glow
Above me, in that stormless sea,
I long to hope that all the woe
Creation knows, is held in thee!

And this shall be my dream to-night;
I'll think the heaven of glorious spheres
Is rolling on its course of light
In endless bliss, through endless years;
I'll think, there's not one world above,
Far as these straining eyes can see,
Where Wisdom ever laughed at Love,
Or Virtue crouched to Infamy;

Where, writhing 'neath the strokes of Fate,
The mangled wretch was forced to smile;
To match his patience 'gainst her hate,

His heart rebellious all the while.
Where Pleasure still will lead to wrong,
And helpless Reason warn in vain;
And Truth is weak, and Treachery strong;
And Joy the surest path to Pain;
And Peace, the lethargy of Grief;
And Hope, a phantom of the soul;
And life, a labour, void and brief;
And Death, the despot of the whole!

Last Words

I knew not 'twas so dire a crime
To say the word, "Adieu;"
But this shall be the only time
My lips or heart shall sue.

That wild hill-side, the winter morn,
The gnarled and ancient tree,
If in your breast they waken scorn,
Shall wake the same in me.

I can forget black eyes and brows,
And lips of falsest charm,
If you forget the sacred vows
Those faithless lips could form.

If hard commands can tame your love,
Or strongest walls can hold,
I would not wish to grieve above
A thing so false and cold.

And there are bosoms bound to mine
With links both tried and strong:
And there are eyes whose lightning shine
Has warmed and blest me long:

Those eyes shall make my only day,
Shall set my spirit free,
And chase the foolish thoughts away
That mourn your memory.

Loud without the wind was roaring

Loud Without The Wind Was Roaring
Loud without the wind was roaring
Through th'autumnal sky;
Drenching wet, the cold rain pouring,
Spoke of winter nigh.
All too like that dreary eve,
Did my exiled spirit grieve.
Grieved at first, but grieved not long,
Sweet—how softly sweet!—it came;
Wild words of an ancient song,
Undefined, without a name.

"It was spring, and the skylark was singing:"
Those words they awakened a spell;
They unlocked a deep fountain, whose springing,
Nor absence, nor distance can quell.

In the gloom of a cloudy November
They uttered the music of May ;
They kindled the perishing ember
Into fervour that could not decay.

Awaken, o'er all my dear moorland,
West-wind, in thy glory and pride!
Oh! call me from valley and lowland,
To walk by the hill-torrent's side!

It is swelled with the first snowy weather;
The rocks they are icy and hoar,
And sullenly waves the long heather,
And the fern leaves are sunny no more.

There are no yellow stars on the mountain
The bluebells have long died away
From the brink of the moss-bedded fountain—
From the side of the wintry brae.
But lovelier than corn-fields all waving
In emerald, and vermeil, and gold,

Are the heights where the north-wind is raving,
And the crags where I wandered of old.

It was morning: the bright sun was beaming;
How sweetly it brought back to me
The time when nor labour nor dreaming
Broke the sleep of the happy and free!

But blithely we rose as the dawn-heaven
Was melting to amber and blue,
And swift were the wings to our feet given,
As we traversed the meadows of dew.

For the moors! For the moors, where the short grass
Like velvet beneath us should lie!
For the moors! For the moors, where each high pass
Rose sunny against the clear sky!

For the moors, where the linnet was trilling
Its song on the old granite stone;
Where the lark, the wild sky-lark, was filling
Every breast with delight like its own!

What language can utter the feeling
Which rose, when in exile afar,
On the brow of a lonely hill kneeling,
I saw the brown heath growing there?

It was scattered and stunted, and told me
That soon even that would be gone:
It whispered, "The grim walls enfold me,
I have bloomed in my last summer's sun."

But not the loved music, whose waking
Makes the soul of the Swiss die away,
Has a spell more adored and heartbreaking
Than, for me, in that blighted heath lay.

The spirit which bent 'neath its power,
How it longed—how it burned to be free!
If I could have wept in that hour,
Those tears had been heaven to me.

Well—well; the sad minutes are moving,
Though loaded with trouble and pain;
And some time the loved and the loving
Shall meet on the mountains again!

Love And Friendship

Love is like the wild rose-briar;
Friendship like the holly-tree.
The holly is dark when the rose-briar blooms,
But which will bloom most constantly?

The wild rose-briar is sweet in spring,
Its summer blossoms scent the air;
Yet wait till winter comes again,
And who will call the wild-briar fair?

Then, scorn the silly rose-wreath now,
And deck thee with the holly's sheen,
That, when December blights thy brow,
He still may leave thy garland green.

My Comforter

Well hast thou spoken, and yet not taught
A feeling strange or new;
Thou hast but roused a latent thought,
A cloud-closed beam of sunshine brought
To gleam in open view.

Deep down, concealed within my soul,
That light lies hid from men;
Yet glows unquenched—though shadows roll,
Its gentle ray cannot control—
About the sullen den.

Was I not vexed, in these gloomy ways
To walk alone so long?
Around me, wretches uttering praise,
Or howling o'er their hopeless days,
And each with Frenzy's tongue;-

A brotherhood of misery,
Their smiles as sad as sighs;
Whose madness daily maddened me,
Distorting into agony
The bliss before my eyes!

So stood I, in Heaven's glorious sun,
And in the glare of Hell;
My spirit drank a mingled tone,
Of seraph's song, and demon's moan;
What my soul bore, my soul alone
Within itself may tell!

Like a soft, air above a sea,
Tossed by the tempest's stir;
A thaw-wind, melting quietly
The snow-drift on some wintry lea;

No: what sweet thing resembles thee,
My thoughtful Comforter?

And yet a little longer speak,
Calm this resentful mood;
And while the savage heart grows meek,
For other token do not seek,
But let the tear upon my cheek
Evince my gratitude!

No Coward Soul Is Mine

No coward soul is mine,
No trembler in the world's storm-troubled sphere:
I see Heaven's glories shine,
And faith shines equal, arming me from fear.

O God within my breast,
Almighty, ever-present Deity!
Life—that in me has rest,
As I—undying Life—have power in thee!

Vain are the thousand creeds
That move men's hearts: unutterably vain;
Worthless as withered weeds,
Or idlest froth amid the boundless main,

To waken doubt in one
Holding so fast by thine infinity;
So surely anchored on
The stedfast rock of immortality.

With wide-embracing love
Thy spirit animates eternal years,
Pervades and broods above,
Changes, sustains, dissolves, creates, and rears.

Though earth and man were gone,
And suns and universes ceased to be,
And Thou were left alone,
Every existence would exist in Thee.

There is not room for Death,
Nor atom that his might could render void:
Thou—THOU art Being and Breath,
And what THOU art may never be destroyed

Plead For Me

Oh, thy bright eyes must answer now,
When Reason, with a scornful brow,
Is mocking at my overthrow!
Oh, thy sweet tongue must plead for me
And tell why I have chosen thee!

Stern Reason is to judgment come,
Arrayed in all her forms of gloom:
Wilt thou, my advocate, be dumb?
No, radiant angel, speak and say,
Why I did cast the world away.

Why I have persevered to shun
The common paths that others run;
And on a strange road journeyed on,
Heedless, alike of wealth and power—
Of glory's wreath and pleasure's flower.

These, once, indeed, seemed Beings Divine;
And they, perchance, heard vows of mine,
And saw my offerings on their shrine;
But careless gifts are seldom prized,
And MINE were worthily despised.

So, with a ready heart, I swore
To seek their altar-stone no more;
And gave my spirit to adore
Thee, ever-present, phantom thing—
My slave, my comrade, and my king.

A slave, because I rule thee still;
Incline thee to my changeful will,
And make thy influence good or ill:
A comrade, for by day and night
Thou art my intimate delight,—

My darling pain that wounds and sears,
And wrings a blessing out from tears
By deadening me to earthly cares;
And yet, a king, though Prudence well
Have taught thy subject to rebel

And am I wrong to worship where
Faith cannot doubt, nor hope despair,
Since my own soul can grant my prayer?
Speak, God of visions, plead for me,
And tell why I have chosen thee!

Remembrance

Cold in the earth—and the deep snow piled above thee,
Far, far, removed, cold in the dreary grave!
Have I forgot, my only Love, to love thee,
Severed at last by Time's all-severing wave?

Now, when alone, do my thoughts no longer hover
Over the mountains, on that northern shore,
Resting their wings where heath and fern-leaves cover
Thy noble heart for ever, ever more?

Cold in the earth—and fifteen wild Decembers,
From those brown hills, have melted into spring:
Faithful, indeed, is the spirit that remembers
After such years of change and suffering!

Sweet Love of youth, forgive, if I forget thee,
While the world's tide is bearing me along;
Other desires and other hopes beset me,
Hopes which obscure, but cannot do thee wrong!

No later light has lightened up my heaven,
No second morn has ever shone for me;
All my life's bliss from thy dear life was given,
All my life's bliss is in the grave with thee.

But, when the days of golden dreams had perished,
And even Despair was powerless to destroy;
Then did I learn how existence could be cherished,
Strengthened, and fed without the aid of joy.

Then did I check the tears of useless passion—
Weaned my young soul from yearning after thine;
Sternly denied its burning wish to hasten
Down to that tomb already more than mine.

And, even yet, I dare not let it languish,
Dare not indulge in memory's rapturous pain;
Once drinking deep of that divinest anguish,
How could I seek the empty world again?

Self-Interrogation

"The evening passes fast away.
'Tis almost time to rest;
What thoughts has left the vanished day,
What feelings in thy breast?

"The vanished day? It leaves a sense
Of labour hardly done;
Of little gained with vast expense—
A sense of grief alone?

"Time stands before the door of Death,
Upbraiding bitterly
And Conscience, with exhaustless breath,
Pours black reproach on me:

"And though I've said that Conscience lies
And Time should Fate condemn;
Still, sad Repentance clouds my eyes,
And makes me yield to them!

"Then art thou glad to seek repose?
Art glad to leave the sea,
And anchor all thy weary woes
In calm Eternity?

"Nothing regrets to see thee go—
Not one voice sobs' farewell;'
And where thy heart has suffered so,
Canst thou desire to dwell?"

"Alas! the countless links are strong
That bind us to our clay;
The loving spirit lingers long,
And would not pass away!

"And rest is sweet, when laurelled fame
Will crown the soldier's crest;
But a brave heart, with a tarnished name,
Would rather fight than rest.

"Well, thou hast fought for many a year,
Hast fought thy whole life through,
Hast humbled Falsehood, trampled Fear;
What is there left to do?

"'Tis true, this arm has hotly striven,
Has dared what few would dare;
Much have I done, and freely given,
But little learnt to bear!

"Look on the grave where thou must sleep
Thy last, and strongest foe;
It is endurance not to weep,
If that repose seem woe.

"The long war closing in defeat—
Defeat serenely borne,—
Thy midnight rest may still be sweet,
And break in glorious morn!"

Shall Earth No More Inspire Thee

Shall earth no more inspire thee,
Thou lonely dreamer now?
Since passion may not fire thee,
Shall nature cease to bow?

Thy mind is ever moving,
In regions dark to thee;
Recall its useless roving,
Come back, and dwell with me.

I know my mountain breezes
Enchant and soothe thee still,
I know my sunshine pleases,
Despite thy wayward will.

When day with evening blending,
Sinks from the summer sky,
I've seen thy spirit bending
In fond idolatry.

I've watched thee every hour;
I know my mighty sway:
I know my magic power
To drive thy griefs away.

Few hearts to mortals given,
On earth so wildly pine;
Yet few would ask a heaven
More like this earth than thine.

Then let my winds caress thee
Thy comrade let me be:
Since nought beside can bless thee,
Return—and dwell with me

Song

The linnet in the rocky dells,
The moor-lark in the air,
The bee among the heather bells
That hide my lady fair:

The wild deer browse above her breast;
The wild birds raise their brood;
And they, her smiles of love caressed,
Have left her solitude!

I ween, that when the grave's dark wall
Did first her form retain,
They thought their hearts could ne'er recall
The light of joy again.

They thought the tide of grief would flow
Unchecked through future years;
But where is all their anguish now,
And where are all their tears?

Well, let them fight for honour's breath,
Or pleasure's shade pursue—
The dweller in the land of death
Is changed and careless too.

And, if their eyes should watch and weep
Till sorrow's source were dry,
She would not, in her tranquil sleep,
Return a single sigh!

Blow, west-wind, by the lonely mound,
And murmur, summer-streams—
There is no need of other sound
To soothe my lady's dreams.

Stanzas

Often rebuked, yet always back returning
To those first feelings that were born with me,
And leaving busy chase of wealth and learning
For idle dreams of things which cannot be:

To-day, I will seek not the shadowy region;
Its unsustaining vastness waxes drear;
And visions rising, legion after legion,
Bring the unreal world too strangely near.

I'll walk, but not in old heroic traces,
And not in paths of high morality,
And not among the half-distinguished faces,
The clouded forms of long-past history.

I'll walk where my own nature would be leading:
It vexes me to choose another guide:
Where the grey flocks in ferny glens are feeding;
Where the wild wind blows on the mountain side.

What have those lonely mountains worth revealing?
More glory and more grief than I can tell:
The earth that wakes one human heart to feeling
Can centre both the worlds of Heaven and Hell.

Stanzas To — —

Well, some may hate, and some may scorn,
And some may quite forget thy name;
But my sad heart must ever mourn
Thy ruined hopes, thy blighted fame!
'Twas thus I thought, an hour ago,
Even weeping o'er that wretch's woe;
One word turned back my gushing tears,
And lit my altered eye with sneers.
Then "Bless the friendly dust," I said,
"That hides thy unlamented head!
Vain as thou wert, and weak as vain,
The slave of Falsehood, Pride, and Pain—
My heart has nought akin to thine;
Thy soul is powerless over mine."
But these were thoughts that vanished too;
Unwise, unholy, and untrue:
Do I despise the timid deer,
Because his limbs are fleet with fear?
Or, would I mock the wolf's death-howl,
Because his form is gaunt and foul?
Or, hear with joy the leveret's cry,
Because it cannot bravely die?
No! Then above his memory
Let Pity's heart as tender be;
Say, "Earth, lie lightly on that breast,
And, kind Heaven, grant that spirit rest!"

Stanzas-

I'll not weep that thou art going to leave me,
There's nothing lovely here;
And doubly will the dark world grieve me,
While thy heart suffers there.

I'll not weep, because the summer's glory
Must always end in gloom;
And, follow out the happiest story—
It closes with a tomb!

And I am weary of the anguish
Increasing winters bear;
Weary to watch the spirit languish
Through years of dead despair.

So, if a tear, when thou art dying,
Should haply fall from me,
It is but that my soul is sighing,
To go and rest with thee.

Stars

Ah! why, because the dazzling sun
Restored our Earth to joy,
Have you departed, every one,
And left a desert sky?

All through the night, your glorious eyes
Were gazing down in mine,
And, with a full heart's thankful sighs,
I blessed that watch divine.

I was at peace, and drank your beams
As they were life to me;
And revelled in my changeful dreams,
Like petrel on the sea.

Thought followed thought, star followed star,
Through boundless regions, on;
While one sweet influence, near and far,
Thrilled through, and proved us one!

Why did the morning dawn to break
So great, so pure, a spell;
And scorch with fire the tranquil cheek,
Where your cool radiance fell?

Blood-red, he rose, and, arrow-straight,
His fierce beams struck my brow;
The soul of nature sprang, elate,
But mine sank sad and low!

My lids closed down, yet through their veil
I saw him, blazing, still,
And steep in gold the misty dale,
And flash upon the hill.

I turned me to the pillow, then,
To call back night, and see
Your worlds of solemn light, again,
Throb with my heart, and me!

It would not do—the pillow glowed,
And glowed both roof and floor;
And birds sang loudly in the wood,
And fresh winds shook the door;

The curtains waved, the wakened flies
Were murmuring round my room,
Imprisoned there, till I should rise,
And give them leave to roam.

Oh, stars, and dreams, and gentle night;
Oh, night and stars, return!
And hide me from the hostile light
That does not warm, but burn;

That drains the blood of suffering men;
Drinks tears, instead of dew;
Let me sleep through his blinding reign,
And only wake with you!

Sympathy

There should be no despair for you
While nightly stars are burning;
While evening pours its silent dew,
And sunshine gilds the morning.
There should be no despair—though tears
May flow down like a river:
Are not the best beloved of years
Around your heart for ever?

They weep, you weep, it must be so;
Winds sigh as you are sighing,
And winter sheds its grief in snow
Where Autumn's leaves are lying:
Yet, these revive, and from their fate
Your fate cannot be parted:
Then, journey on, if not elate,
Still, NEVER broken-hearted!

The Bluebell

The Bluebell is the sweetest flower
That waves in summer air:
Its blossoms have the mightiest power
To soothe my spirit's care.

There is a spell in purple heath
Too wildly, sadly dear;
The violet has a fragrant breath,
But fragrance will not cheer,

The trees are bare, the sun is cold,
And seldom, seldom seen;
The heavens have lost their zone of gold,
And earth her robe of green.

And ice upon the glancing stream
Has cast its sombre shade;
And distant hills and valleys seem
In frozen mist arrayed.

The Bluebell cannot charm me now,
The heath has lost its bloom;
The violets in the glen below,
They yield no sweet perfume.

But, though I mourn the sweet Bluebell,
'Tis better far away;
I know how fast my tears would swell
To see it smile to-day.

For, oh! when chill the sunbeams fall
Adown that dreary sky,
And gild yon dank and darkened wall
With transient brilliancy;

How do I weep, how do I pine
For the time of flowers to come,
And turn me from that fading shine,
To mourn the fields of home!

The Elder's Rebuke

"Listen! When your hair, like mine,
Takes a tint of silver gray;
When your eyes, with dimmer shine,
Watch life's bubbles float away:

When you, young man, have borne like me
The weary weight of sixty-three,
Then shall penance sore be paid
For those hours so wildly squandered;
And the words that now fall dead
On your ear, be deeply pondered—
Pondered and approved at last:
But their virtue will be past!

"Glorious is the prize of Duty,
Though she be 'a serious power';
Treacherous all the lures of Beauty,
Thorny bud and poisonous flower!

"Mirth is but a mad beguiling
Of the golden-gifted time;
Love—a demon-meteor, wiling
Heedless feet to gulfs of crime.

"Those who follow earthly pleasure,
Heavenly knowledge will not lead;
Wisdom hides from them her treasure,
Virtue bids them evil-speed!

"Vainly may their hearts repenting.
Seek for aid in future years;
Wisdom, scorned, knows no relenting;
Virtue is not won by fears."

Thus spake the ice-blooded elder gray;
The young man scoffed as he turned away,
Turned to the call of a sweet lute's measure,
Waked by the lightsome touch of pleasure:
Had he ne'er met a gentler teacher,
Woe had been wrought by that pitiless preacher.

The Lady To Her Guitar

For him who struck thy foreign string,
I ween this heart has ceased to care;
Then why dost thou such feelings bring
To my sad spirit—old Guitar?

It is as if the warm sunlight
In some deep glen should lingering stay,
When clouds of storm, or shades of night,
Have wrapt the parent orb away.

It is as if the glassy brook
Should image still its willows fair,
Though years ago the woodman's stroke
Laid low in dust their Dryad-hair.

Even so, Guitar, thy magic tone
Hath moved the tear and waked the sigh:
Hath bid the ancient torrent moan,
Although its very source is dry.

The Night-wind

In summer's mellow midnight,
A cloudless moon shone through
Our open parlour window,
And rose-trees wet with dew.

I sat in silent musing;
The soft wind waved my hair;
It told me heaven was glorious,
And sleeping earth was fair.

I needed not its breathing
To bring such thoughts to me;
But still it whispered lowly,
How dark the woods will be!

"The thick leaves in my murmur
Are rustling like a dream,
And all their myriad voices
Instinct with spirit seem."

I said, "Go, gentle singer,
Thy wooing voice is kind:
But do not think its music
Has power to reach my mind.

"Play with the scented flower,
The young tree's supple bough,
And leave my human feelings
In their own course to flow."

The wanderer would not heed me;
Its kiss grew warmer still.
"O come!" it sighed so sweetly;
"I'll win thee 'gainst thy will.

"Were we not friends from childhood?
Have I not loved thee long?
As long as thou, the solemn night,
Whose silence wakes my song.

"And when thy heart is resting
Beneath the church-aisle stone,
I shall have time for mourning,
And THOU for being alone."

The Old Stoic

Riches I hold in light esteem,
And Love I laugh to scorn;
And lust of fame was but a dream,
That vanished with the morn:

And if I pray, the only prayer
That moves my lips for me
Is, "Leave the heart that now I bear,
And give me liberty!"

Yes, as my swift days near their goal:
'Tis all that I implore ;
In life and death a chainless soul,
With courage to endure.

The Philosopher

Enough of thought, philosopher!
Too long hast thou been dreaming
Unlightened, in this chamber drear,
While summer's sun is beaming!
Space-sweeping soul, what sad refrain
Concludes thy musings once again?

"Oh, for the time when I shall sleep
Without identity.
And never care how rain may steep,
Or snow may cover me!
No promised heaven, these wild desires
Could all, or half fulfil;
No threatened hell, with quenchless fires,
Subdue this quenchless will!"

"So said I, and still say the same;
Still, to my death, will say—
Three gods, within this little frame,
Are warring night; and day;
Heaven could not hold them all, and yet
They all are held in me;
And must be mine till I forget
My present entity!
Oh, for the time, when in my breast
Their struggles will be o'er!
Oh, for the day, when I shall rest,
And never suffer more!"

"I saw a spirit, standing, man,
Where thou dost stand—an hour ago,
And round his feet three rivers ran,
Of equal depth, and equal flow—
A golden stream—and one like blood;
And one like sapphire seemed to be;

52

But, where they joined their triple flood
It tumbled in an inky sea
The spirit sent his dazzling gaze
Down through that ocean's gloomy night;
Then, kindling all, with sudden blaze,
The glad deep sparkled wide and bright—
White as the sun, far, far more fair
Than its divided sources were!"

"And even for that spirit, seer,
I've watched and sought my life-time long;
Sought him in heaven, hell, earth, and air,
An endless search, and always wrong.
Had I but seen his glorious eye
ONCE light the clouds that wilder me;
I ne'er had raised this coward cry
To cease to think, and cease to be;

I ne'er had called oblivion blest,
Nor stretching eager hands to death,
Implored to change for senseless rest
This sentient soul, this living breath—
Oh, let me die—that power and will
Their cruel strife may close;
And conquered good, and conquering ill
Be lost in one repose!"

The Prisoner

A fragment.

In the dungeon-crypts idly did I stray,
Reckless of the lives wasting there away;
"Draw the ponderous bars! open, Warder stern!"
He dared not say me nay—the hinges harshly turn.

"Our guests are darkly lodged," I whisper'd, gazing through
The vault, whose grated eye showed heaven more gray than blue;
(This was when glad Spring laughed in awaking pride;)
"Ay, darkly lodged enough!" returned my sullen guide.

Then, God forgive my youth; forgive my careless tongue;
I scoffed, as the chill chains on the damp flagstones rung:
"Confined in triple walls, art thou so much to fear,
That we must bind thee down and clench thy fetters here?"

The captive raised her face; it was as soft and mild
As sculptured marble saint, or slumbering unwean'd child;
It was so soft and mild, it was so sweet and fair,
Pain could not trace a line, nor grief a shadow there!

The captive raised her hand and pressed it to her brow;
"I have been struck," she said, "and I am suffering now;
Yet these are little worth, your bolts and irons strong;
And, were they forged in steel, they could not hold me long."

Hoarse laughed the jailor grim: "Shall I be won to hear;
Dost think, fond, dreaming wretch, that I shall grant thy prayer?
Or, better still, wilt melt my master's heart with groans?
Ah! sooner might the sun thaw down these granite stones.

"My master's voice is low, his aspect bland and kind,
But hard as hardest flint the soul that lurks behind;
And I am rough and rude, yet not more rough to see

Than is the hidden ghost that has its home in me."

About her lips there played a smile of almost scorn,
"My friend," she gently said, "you have not heard me mourn;
When you my kindred's lives, MY lost life, can restore,
Then may I weep and sue,—but never, friend, before!

"Still, let my tyrants know, I am not doomed to wear
Year after year in gloom, and desolate despair;
A messenger of Hope comes every night to me,
And offers for short life, eternal liberty.

"He comes with western winds, with evening's wandering airs,
With that clear dusk of heaven that brings the thickest stars.
Winds take a pensive tone, and stars a tender fire,
And visions rise, and change, that kill me with desire.

"Desire for nothing known in my maturer years,
When Joy grew mad with awe, at counting future tears.
When, if my spirit's sky was full of flashes warm,
I knew not whence they came, from sun or thunder-storm.

"But, first, a hush of peace—a soundless calm descends;
The struggle of distress, and fierce impatience ends;
Mute music soothes my breast—unuttered harmony,
That I could never dream, till Earth was lost to me.

"Then dawns the Invisible; the Unseen its truth reveals;
My outward sense is gone, my inward essence feels:
Its wings are almost free—its home, its harbour found,
Measuring the gulph, it stoops and dares the final bound,

"Oh I dreadful is the check—intense the agony—
When the ear begins to hear, and the eye begins to see;
When the pulse begins to throb, the brain to think again;
The soul to feel the flesh, and the flesh to feel the chain.

"Yet I would lose no sting, would wish no torture less;
The more that anguish racks, the earlier it will bless;
And robed in fires of hell, or bright with heavenly shine,
If it but herald death, the vision is divine!"

She ceased to speak, and we, unanswering, turned to go—
We had no further power to work the captive woe:
Her cheek, her gleaming eye, declared that man had given
A sentence, unapproved, and overruled by Heaven.

The Two Children

Heavy hangs the rain-drop
From the burdened spray;
Heavy broods the damp mist
On uplands far away.

Heavy looms the dull sky,
Heavy rolls the sea;
And heavy throbs the young heart
Beneath that lonely tree.

Never has a blue streak
Cleft the clouds since morn;
Never has his grim fate
Smiled since he was born.

Frowning on the infant,
Shadowing childhood's joy
Guardian-angel knows not
That melancholy boy.

Day is passing swiftly
Its sad and sombre prime;
Boyhood sad is merging
In sadder manhood's time:

All the flowers are praying
For sun, before they close,
And he prays too—unconscious—
That sunless human rose.

Blossom—that the west-wind
Has never wooed to blow,
Scentless are thy petals,
Thy dew is cold as snow!

Soul—where kindred kindness,
No early promise woke,
Barren is thy beauty,
As weed upon a rock.

Wither—soul and blossom!
You both were vainly given;
Earth reserves no blessing
For the unblest of heaven!

Child of delight, with sun-bright hair,
And sea-blue, sea-deep eyes!
Spirit of bliss! What brings thee here
Beneath these sullen skies?

Thou shouldst live in eternal spring,
Where endless day is never dim;
Why, Seraph, has thine erring wing
Wafted thee down to weep with him?

"Ah! not from heaven am I descended,
Nor do I come to mingle tears;
But sweet is day, though with shadows blended;
And, though clouded, sweet are youthful years.

"I—the image of light and gladness—
Saw and pitied that mournful boy,
And I vowed—if need were—to share his sadness,
And give to him my sunny joy.

"Heavy and dark the night is closing;
Heavy and dark may its biding be:
Better for all from grief reposing,
And better for all who watch like me—

"Watch in love by a fevered pillow,
Cooling the fever with pity's balm

Safe as the petrel on tossing billow,
Safe in mine own soul's golden calm!

"Guardian-angel he lacks no longer;
Evil fortune he need not fear:
Fate is strong, but love is stronger;
And MY love is truer than angel-care."

The Visionary

Silent is the house: all are laid asleep:
One alone looks out o'er the snow-wreaths deep,
Watching every cloud, dreading every breeze
That whirls the wildering drift, and bends the groaning trees.

Cheerful is the hearth, soft the matted floor;
Not one shivering gust creeps through pane or door;
The little lamp burns straight, its rays shoot strong and far:
I trim it well, to be the wanderer's guiding-star.

Frown, my haughty sire! chide, my angry dame!
Set your slaves to spy; threaten me with shame:
But neither sire nor dame, nor prying serf shall know,
What angel nightly tracks that waste of frozen snow.

What I love shall come like visitant of air,
Safe in secret power from lurking human snare;
What loves me, no word of mine shall e'er betray,
Though for faith unstained my life must forfeit pay

Burn, then, little lamp; glimmer straight and clear—
Hush! a rustling wing stirs, methinks, the air:
He for whom I wait, thus ever comes to me;
Strange Power! I trust thy might; trust thou my constancy.

The Wanderer From The Fold

How few, of all the hearts that loved,
Are grieving for thee now;
And why should mine to-night be moved
With such a sense of woe?

Too often thus, when left alone,
Where none my thoughts can see,
Comes back a word, a passing tone
From thy strange history.

Sometimes I seem to see thee rise,
A glorious child again;
All virtues beaming from thine eyes
That ever honoured men:

Courage and truth, a generous breast
Where sinless sunshine lay:
A being whose very presence blest
Like gladsome summer-day.

O, fairly spread thy early sail,
And fresh, and pure, and free,
Was the first impulse of the gale
Which urged life's wave for thee!

Why did the pilot, too confiding,
Dream o'er that ocean's foam,
And trust in Pleasure's careless guiding
To bring his vessel home?

For well he knew what dangers frowned,
What mists would gather, dim;
What rocks and shelves, and sands lay round
Between his port and him.

The very brightness of the sun
The splendour of the main,
The wind which bore him wildly on
Should not have warned in vain.

An anxious gazer from the shore—
I marked the whitening wave,
And wept above thy fate the more
Because—I could not save.

It recks not now, when all is over:
But yet my heart will be
A mourner still, though friend and lover
Have both forgotten thee!

To Imagination

When weary with the long day's care,
And earthly change from pain to pain,
And lost, and ready to despair,
Thy kind voice calls me back again:
Oh, my true friend! I am not lone,
While then canst speak with such a tone!

So hopeless is the world without;
The world within I doubly prize;
Thy world, where guile, and hate, and doubt,
And cold suspicion never rise;
Where thou, and I, and Liberty,
Have undisputed sovereignty.

What matters it, that all around
Danger, and guilt, and darkness lie,
If but within our bosom's bound
We hold a bright, untroubled sky,
Warm with ten thousand mingled rays
Of suns that know no winter days?

Reason, indeed, may oft complain
For Nature's sad reality,
And tell the suffering heart how vain
Its cherished dreams must always be;
And Truth may rudely trample down
The flowers of Fancy, newly-blown:

But thou art ever there, to bring
The hovering vision back, and breathe
New glories o'er the blighted spring,
And call a lovelier Life from Death.
And whisper, with a voice divine,
Of real worlds, as bright as thine.

I trust not to thy phantom bliss,
Yet, still, in evening's quiet hour,
With never-failing thankfulness,
I welcome thee, Benignant Power;
Sure solacer of human cares,
And sweeter hope, when hope despairs!

Warning And Reply

In the earth—the earth—thou shalt be laid,
A grey stone standing over thee;
Black mould beneath thee spread,
And black mould to cover thee.

"Well—there is rest there,
So fast come thy prophecy;
The time when my sunny hair
Shall with grass roots entwined be."

But cold—cold is that resting-place,
Shut out from joy and liberty,
And all who loved thy living face
Will shrink from it shudderingly,

"Not so. HERE the world is chill,
And sworn friends fall from me:
But THERE—they will own me still,
And prize my memory."

Farewell, then, all that love,
All that deep sympathy:
Sleep on: Heaven laughs above,
Earth never misses thee.

Turf-sod and tombstone drear
Part human company;
One heart breaks only—here,
But that heart was worthy thee!

CPSIA information can be obtained
at www.ICGtesting.com
Printed in the USA
LVHW091630140821
695327LV00010B/1251